JohnYamrus

SELECTED

POEMS

Edited and with an Introduction by Mish Murphy

Concrete Mist Press

York, PA 17403

USA

Temple1130@aol.com

Copyright © 2021 by John Yamrus

Introduction Copyright © 2021 by Mish Murphy

First Edition

Cover art: Mish (Eileen Murphy)

Edited by Heath Brougher and Mish

Cover design: Concrete Mist Press and Mish

ISBN: 978-1-7368935-1-7

Manufactured in the United States of America

TABLE OF CONTENTS

PART 1	1
my dogs	3
when	4
it's always something...	5
the [weeds]	7
after the reading,	8
sooner or later	9
that was when she went	11
i've got	13
dunno	14
she loves daisies	15
he [couldn't have]	17
at the doctor's	18
i swear,	19
when i walked into	20
it was back in	22
there is	25
a pretty good poem	26
look, man (he says to me),...	28
i spent the night	30
the voices	32
if [they're / telling you]	33
there has to be	34
horrified,	36
"this poem's a mess"	37
the boring poet	38
the cigarette	40
Henry always	41
did i ever tell you	44
you [are / a bowl of popcorn]	46
the publisher	48

i don't get it	50
puke-green	51
Dan and Carol	52
look at	55
Landon	56
the first	57
Martin accused me	58
okay, Mr. Death, you win...	59
since before	61
object lesson:	62
"i really don't drink much,"	64
he died	66
for years now	67
i don't know what it was	69
we [are / less]	72
approaching 70:	73
the knees	75
i bought the new	78
they tell me	80
now that Bukowski's dead	82
this poem	84
PART 2	87
"write a poem about *THAT*,"	89
i was reading	90
the miracle	92
my old dog's gone deaf	93
i ask	95
weep	97
Jesus Christ!	98
don't put me	99
why i'm not Buk...	101
if [being / dead is]	103
the great writer	104

twice	105
expect much	107
I've	109
he [said / he / did / it]	110
red:	111
picture this:	112
it was	114
even my clothes	116
you [are a single]	117
if [you think]	118
a word to the wise:	119
a hurt that scars the landscape of the soul	120
there	121
he spent	122
Murray knew he	123
and all the sick, perverted	125
Screaming Jay Hawkins	128
somebody take my picture, quick!	129
i was sitting in a corner	131
contrary	134
the dog	135
Tony	136
the next question	138
he clued her in	139
the hell with	140
when i	141
memories	143
even	144
i worked in a phone room once...	145
i've been shit on...	148
after midnight	150
and	151
do not	152
it's time	153
the great	154

if [you are the first]	155
she works	156
the apartment	158
all	159
he [knew it]	160
her	161
old records	162
for	164
when i was a kid	166
the [thing]	168
silly me	169
the editor asked	171
i am not a writer	173
Tony wasn't very	174
after	176
PART 3	179
i remember	181
this	182
she said:	183
he had this thing	184
if [you / can't]	187
most days	188
even if	190
nothing	191
one of my first	192
my friend Bill	194
"stop opening things with your teeth,"	197
first	199
the streets	200
tell me	201
Ricky Lee	202
sometimes	204
Jesus, it	205

bullets	206
they [both]	207
the neighbor's dog	208
no,	210
it was	211
give me	213
her [nakedness]	214
after working in	215
after the reading	216
looking	218
my	219
reluctantly,	220
i never played	221
don't	222
the [sad]	223
Hardy	224
i love you	225
i'm	226
Les Ismore	227
midnight's	228
it was near sunset	229
the fire...	234
do not	235
my friend Stanley hated the sun	236
after work	237
he [was / obsessed]	239
New York just	240
until	242
this chair	244
a review	245
Bukowski's property	246
he [sat]	247
the [geese]	248
give me poetry	249
how	250

PART 4	253
i wanna tell you a story...	255
miracles	259
a really bad poem about a real good dog...	260
if [you ask]	262
Dr. Lambert	263
i was out	265
when [asked / why]	267
i think [the time that]	268
he'd play	269
after my colonoscopy	270
Rick	271
Henry Miller	274
Bukowski started his novel	276
Randolph was an ass...	278
when i was a kid, i	280
tonight	283
she could have been great	285
i sat in the sun room	287
Tony the Lip	291
he [didn't]	293
it's too late	294
it's all too safe	295
poetry	297
right now,	298
this	299
my dog doesn't care much	300
message read	302
i was just now	303
he looked at me and	304
doing the laundry,	306
driving toward Lancaster,	307
"Dear John:	309
the other day he	312

his book,	313
his face	315
on reading some of	316
she said: [touch]	318
i'm a sucker for	319
she [looked at]	321
my car battery died and	322
find	323
i'll	324
i think [i was]	325
the neighbor died today	328
she said [she / was pleased]	329
i [saw / the ghost]	331
my [cries]	332
the doorbell rang	333
if [you want]	335
i'm getting mean	336
the only thing	338
she said [you think]	339
there's a poem	340
he asked me [how do i]	341
Q	342
i	343
pass	344
PART 5	347
endure	349
"endure" [art print]	351
ACKNOWLEDGEMENTS	353
OTHER WORKS BY JOHN YAMRUS	355
ABOUT THE AUTHOR	357
ABOUT THE EDITOR	359

DEDICATION

This book is dedicated to Moses Yanes and Dan McGinley and Bernt Danielsson and Alan Burgis and Linda King and R.D. Armstrong and Wolf Carstens and Janne Karlsson and Heath Brougher and all those other crazy publishers whose names would fill this page and beyond, who often put up their own money and sacrificed health, hearth and home to keep me in print. It's also dedicated to Kathy, who always was and always will be.

—John Yamrus

INTRODUCTION
by Mish Murphy

John Yamrus's poems are a lot like pistachios or potato chips: you can't stop at one.

The poems in *Selected Poems* are a binge-worthy feast[1], featuring the best poetry by a master of postmodern minimalism, a genre almost singlehandedly and unintentionally created by John Yamrus.

John has been writing poems since 1970. He's published over 2,500 individual poems and 28 books of poetry, plus two novels, three memoirs, and a children's book. Although he might have once been considered a "cult favorite," he's now become mainstream.

This new status as a mainstream poet—and the respectability that implies—isn't something John has sought; in fact, it's just the opposite:

> **do not**
>
> force
> your tired,
> tarnished bonhomie
>
> on
> my
> soul

---

[1] I was inspired by Michael Zielinski's Introduction to *Small Talk* where he calls John's poetry "a sumptuous smorgasbord of profound simplicity."

i
will not

have
it

(p. 152)

I got to know John while I was in the process of writing a review of one of his books, *As Real as Rain.* We became friends, I think, because he and I are both fervent, shameless dog lovers. More recently. John and I collaborated on the children's book *Phoebe and Ito are dogs,* which he wrote and I illustrated. We've been "dog buddies" and "poetry buddies" ever since.

Selected Poems is a collection of John Yamrus's poetry from across his long career. It's a huge book with over 300 pages of poetry. Even so, we were picky when selecting poems. Given the output of such a consistently prolific writer (for some reason, John *hates* being called a poet), there was an enormous pool of high-quality work to choose from.

John's poetry is super-diverse and includes poems that explore funny or sad anecdotes about his encounters with wannabe poets, book reviewers, and interviewers. There are also poems about people who suicide and/or who drink; there are love poems for his wife, dog poems, and little ironic gems about the nature of poetry, writing, and life. Take, for example, this one:

how

were
we
to know

we
were
happy?

(p. 250)

In this poem, John manages to be poetic while keeping to his minimalist style. He is an expert at packing multiple nuances into a few words. And, above all, this poem seems simple and easy to understand, the key word being *seems*.

Although the book is divided into five parts, the poems are not classified or sorted into categories like "dog poems" or "writing poems." Yamrus resists being labeled and objects to his poems' being labeled. Instead, the poems in *Selected Poems* are arranged to provide the reader with an entertaining, diverse poetic playlist in each of the five sections of the book.

The poems in *Selected Poems* are fresh, crunchy, and satisfying. A John Yamrus poem looks and sounds all-natural. It slides down your tongue and into your system with its slim, simple language. And it may produce beneficial side effects such as laughter and/or tears.

Because these poems are generally short and may be read quickly, there is a tendency to dismiss them as lightweight or inconsequential. But therein lies their secret and their beauty: the poems don't have to say a lot to mean a lot. At the end of the day, isn't that the essence of poetry?

And then, sometimes John's poems are just plain nutty, a result of his Zen mindset[2] meeting his noir sensibility. I love it when John's speaker gets absurd, as in this piece:

i remember

the
porch

the
grey paint

the
swing

the
flowers

the
awning

and
the hedges.

my

---

[2] I credit Mark Statman with being the first to call John a "Zen" poet. See Statman's Introduction to John's collection *Alchemy*.

god,

i
remember

the
hedges.

(p. 181)

As editor of *Selected Poems,* I made sure the book included
John's iconic one-word poem "endure," which happens to
be a personal favorite of mine (this and another poem, "my
dogs").

At one point in the distant past, John had to put up with
snickering from certain literary types who judged "endure"
harshly: "That's not a real poem."

There's an old saying, *He who laughs last, laughs best.* As
a result of this overblown controversy, "endure" became
famous (or infamous, really); and the poem endured years
of being scrutinized and patronized, only to emerge
vindicated.

Now there is even an illustrated art print with the poem
"endure" on it along with John's face in the background; it
was featured in a recent documentary film.

I interpret the poem "endure" as expressing John Yamrus's
philosophy of writing: how it's important to work at your
writing consistently day after day, year after year. Such
devotion, such endurance, is responsible for the high-

quality body of work he has been accumulating since he started writing poetry 51 years ago.

Yamrus has sometimes been called an "outlaw" poet, but his work resists easy classification. His poetry is based on the great poetry of the past while using new flavors derived from his own head. His roots are in the works of Bukowski and Kerouac, and he's been influenced by many jazz greats, especially Miles Davis and Thelonious Monk.

John grew up in a small coal mining town in Pennsylvania. His father, who had aspired to a baseball career and briefly played in the minor leagues, worked in the mines. John knew tragedy at an early age when his dad suddenly died from a heart attack when John was 11. John went on to marry his high school sweetheart, and they are still happily married today.

I believe John's "Kathy" poems (my label, not his) are among the finest in this "best of" collection. They're tender, full of unwavering faith in their relationship, and yet offer, perhaps for texture, a pleasant twinge of something bittersweet—nostalgia, maybe? Here's an example:

after

the
rain,

reading Kerouac,

listening
to Cole Porter

playing quiet in the room,

there's
even birds
singing outside the window.

the
only thing
missing here

is
you.

(p. 176)

All in all, the publication of *Selected Poems* establishes
John Yamrus's membership in the ranks of the most
important contemporary poets. It brings together his best
work from across five decades—sharp-witted, entertaining,
and fearless.

However, you need to realize that once you start reading
this book, you may not be able to stop. It may be too late
for that. You might even find yourself binge-reading.
And one of the small gems in *Selected Poems* may apply:

pass

the

lightning,
please.

(p. 344)

PART 1

my dogs

bark at the neighbors,
bark at the UPS man,
bark at cars
and kids on bicycles.

they bark at the tv,
the radio
and the stereo.

they bark at
the vacuum,
the dust mop
and the broom.

they bark at
anyone
who enters the house
uninvited.

and
when they're not barking,
they're sitting there,
waiting
for something
to bark at.

good dogs.

when

i
sent
the magazine

a
poem
that was
one word long,

he
said
what the
hell is this?

i
said

art.

it's always something...

like
this morning...

my dog
went and
fell in the pool.

it was 5AM, and
i let her out and lay on
the couch and fell asleep.

then,
i hear Kathy yelling:

"what's wrong with Abby?"

and i listen
and the poor dog's screaming,
like she got hit by a car.

i run into
the kitchen
and look out back
and she's in the pool.

proof positive
that all dogs can't swim.

i'm sure that
half the neighborhood
heard her howling

5

and was looking
out their windows...

yet, there i was,
in my underwear,
pulling a wet
and crying dog
from the pool.

but i didn't care.
the trade was
more than
fair.

my dignity
for her
life.

i certainly
owed her one,
for sure,

because that dog
with her great, grey eyes
and absolutely
crazy ways

manages to
save my
life

every single
day.

the

weeds
lie
in
piles
on
the
ground.

yes,
they
will
grow
back.

that's
what
weeds
do.

after the reading,

a
reporter
for the student paper

asked me
what career i would take

if
i wasn't a writer.

i
looked at him

and said:
at this point in my life
i guess porn star is out of the question.

the
poor kid
looked at me.

he
didn't
know what to say.

neither did i.

sooner or later

it
catches up with you.

no matter
how well
you run the race,

it catches up with you.

and you're left
standing alone,
blindfolded,
with your back
against the wall

as the guy
at the other end of the yard
starts counting down...

"Ready..."

the only thing that matters
as he continues
to count...

"Aim..."

the only thing in the world
that's left to you
is to hold your head

and face
the

"Fire!".

that was when she went

absolutely
bat-shit crazy on him,

throwing things,
kicking the walls,
sometimes even
setting his clothes
on fire.

she didn't do it
very often,
but,

when
she did,

it
sure was
something.

for seventeen years
he kept his
mouth
shut,

and
put up
with it.

if you
asked him

he'd say
he always will.

besides,
it could have been worse.

she could have
married

someone
else.

i've got

this hair
on my nose,

near
the tip,

and
no matter
how often

i
cut it,

or
pluck it,

it
keeps
coming back.

now,
that's just
damned admirable...

don't
you think?

dunno

got
no answers

got
no questions

got
no whys

and
got no
wherefores

all i got
is me

me
and the
poem

and
what,

my
friend,

have
you?

she loves daisies

i'm not
very good
at remembering that.

on those
rare occasions
when i DO
bring flowers
it's usually
roses,
or those 3 dollar bundles
from the market.

never daisies.

and never
at the right moment.

it's usually
for something i did,

forgot
to do,

or should have done.

and
when it IS
daisies...

when i'm

putting them

in a vase
and adding water,

i can't help
thinking
about

bees.

he

couldn't
have

he
shouldn't have

but,
he did

at the doctor's

i got
the results
of my bloodwork.

he said
my numbers
are off the charts,

and
my kidneys
are processing blood

"like a racehorse."

he called it
"insane."

he said everything
was excellent

and that
whatever i was doing,
i should continue to do the same.

so,
on the way home,
i stopped and bought a case of wine.

i swear,

one of
these days

i'll
get it

right.

when i walked into

the waiting room
at the dentist's
there was only
one seat open.

i took it,
grabbed a copy of *Newsweek*
and tried
to hide my face.

but,
before i even
opened the magazine
this guy on my right
leans over
and starts talking"

"...used to play guitar once...

years ago,
when i was a kid.

i was pretty good at it, too!"

knowing it was useless,
i put down the magazine
and turned toward him.

he was
an ordinary kind of guy...

maybe 50.

"it was
a great way
to pick up women.

i met
all sorts of women
when i was playing guitar.

that's how
i met my wife."

just then
they called my name
and i stood up.

he reached for my magazine
and said:

"yep,
it's been years
since i played guitar...

now
i play
second fiddle."

it was back in

high school...i
was a senior, playing
a very mediocre
third base.

i didn't play much
because
to tell the truth
i wasn't very good.

also on the team was
this sophomore,
McGinley.

he was even
worse,

but he had
the heart
i lacked.

he ran everything out
at full speed...

even in
practice.

slow as he was,
he'd be gritting his teeth,

brow furrowed

and sweating

and he'd
run to first base

hard.

he ran hard
and

he practiced
hard

and
took all the
crap we threw at him.

we laughed,
when he'd fall
and we'd yell "eat 'em up,
McGinley!"

but, every single time
he got back up
and kept on
running.

pretty soon,
"eat 'em up, McGinley"
became a rallying cry
on the team.

that was

a long time ago

and i have no clue
what's happened to him,

but i sure as hell hope
that slow-running,
slope-shouldered,
over-weight
bastard of a guy

can still
eat 'em
up.

there is

nothing
better

than
the smell

of a
sleeping dog.

a pretty good poem

popped
into my head.

i
was
out back
in the hot tub.

it was
near midnight

and
i just
poured a
glass of wine.

i
wasn't
about to get out,

so i
repeated it
over and over
in my head, until

i
had it
memorized.

and
i hope

you
like it.

look, man, (he says to me)...

i don't know nothing
about poetry.

never have.

never will.

i can't tell
a quatrain
from a
freight train

but, if i were
to write me a poem,

i'd
do one
about
that girl
over there.

she's just
bad news
waiting to happen.

yep,
if i ever wrote me a poem,

it'd
be about her...

look
at her...

ain't she
something?

why,
she's just...

just...

a
thorn
without
the rose.

i spent the night

sitting in my chair
listening to this
set of tapes
i bought
earlier
in the
day...

old radio shows from the
1940s and '50s...

hardboiled detectives.

Philip Marlowe,

Boston Blackie,

Johnny Dollar.

tough guys
who

knew their way
around a knife
and a gun
and a
dame.

men
who talked fast

and
walked slow...

men
of wit and courage

and
charm.

for three hours
i listened...

then,
tired,
i finally took
one last slug of beer

and walked out
onto the back porch,

hoping
that someone
would be stupid

or foolish

or
desperate enough

to try and
sneak up
and slug me
from behind.

the voices

in
his
head

told him
he'd find god

at
Taco Bell.

he
didn't.

but,
he did
find Janey.

the
voices
approved.

if

they're
telling you
your writing's good,

don't
believe them.

what
they're saying
is you're giving them
something they've seen before.

don't
be safe.

fall
on your face.

try
something new.

try
something new.

try.

there has to be

an end
to toothaches

and
headaches.

and
hemorrhoids

and
pimples.

there
has to be

an end
to jobs with no heart

and
people
with no soul.

there
has to be
an end to
all the tiny pains

that
wear you down
and leave you sick
and staring at the wall

at 3 a.m. on a Saturday night.

there
has to be.

but
i don't

see it.

horrified,

she
said:

oh, no,
i never drink!

to
which
he said:

that
explains

a
lot.

"this poem's a mess."

(he says to me)

"it
violates
every rule
i ever heard of.

there's
not one thing in it
that's even remotely familiar."

thanks,
i was hoping you'd say that.

the boring poet

in every single poem
quotes in Greek
just to let you know
he knows.

he's
also prone
to dropping names
(the more obscure, the better).

and
it's all
so lifeless

and so boring.

he's
all that's wrong
with poetry today.

my
advice to him
would be to open up his veins

and
tell the truth.

leave a little of your life
on the page.

do that,

and you can
even get away with it

in Greek.

the cigarette

burned
low,

and
he leaned
over to smother it
on the table near the bed.

as he
pressed the stub

in
the tray,

he
heard

the
knock
on the door.

Henry always

talked
so smooth and cool.

nothing
seemed to
bother him.

Henry
always had it together.

he always knew
what to say,

when to
say it,

and
who to
say it to.

Henry
was cool.

i always hated Henry.

i hated
the smugness.

i hated
everything about him.

i hated his
short, chubby fingers.

i hated
his gray, wrinkled pants.

and,
most of all,

i hated Henry
just for being Henry.

and then,
late this afternoon,

i was
driving route 422,

just past
the dirty book store,

and i
saw Henry walking out.

he had a
package under his arm.

he looked
scared and confused.

he didn't
look like Henry at all.

i honked the horn.

he
turned.

i waved.

and,
for the briefest moment,

i
didn't think
Henry was such a bad guy

after all.

did i ever tell you

about the time
Linda said i was good,
but that i'd never be
Bukowski?

Linda
was a poet.

one of Bukowski's
girlfriends
in the '70s.

for a while
she edited and published
a pretty decent little magazine.

she wrote to me saying
that she loved my poems...

actually, it's been so long now
i really don't remember
if she loved them
or liked them,
but, it doesn't matter...

she said that i was good,
but, i would never be great...

because i wasn't
mad.

Bukowski (she said) was mad...
and he was
great.

i wrote back
saying that she was right...

Bukowski IS mad
and Bukowski IS great,

but, if one of the qualifications
for being mad
and being great
was having to put up with the likes of her,
then i'd be more than happy
to settle for what i am
and what i'm
going to be.

that was 30 years ago,
and do you know what?

i'm still not mad
and i'm still not
great...

but, every now and then,
when the moon's just right
i'm not
half bad.

you

are
a bowl of popcorn,

a slim volume of poems

and laughter
during a moment of silence.

you are
pink bubble gum,

a damn fool

and the only
person in the world
i care about.

you are
a clock with no hands,

a blue bedroom

and a
twenty-dollar bill.

you
refuse to accept
the inevitable.

you own
way too many dresses

and you don't
shoot pool.

you are
as uncomplaining
as the sea.

ultimately,

no one
can put you
into words...

not

even

me.

the publisher

wanted
to put out a book
of mine
and he wanted
it
to be out by
a certain date
and i didn't
have
enough
poems
to fill it
up
so i
panicked
and walked
the streets
looking
for something
to happen
waiting
for someone to
say something
interesting
and it
just wasn't
happening
so i
figured
i'd have to
take the

bull by the
horns
and do it
myself
and
i thought i'd
take
a cue
from Bob
Dylan
so
i
built a
fire on
Main Street
and
shot it
full of
holes.

i don't get it.

the
poems
seem to come

easier now.

there were times
when it felt like
the beginning
of the end,

and
the poems
scratched and
clawed and fought.

now,
they just lie there,

smiling,

waiting for me
to stick it
in.

puke-green

was
his favorite color.

it
was also
his favorite word

(or,
words, if
you wanted to
get technical about it).

anyway,
it was kinda sorta fitting
that he had already turned his
favorite color that Sunday morning

when
they found him
face down under the Penn Street Bridge.

Dan and Carol

had an apartment
downtown.

this was right around the time
my first book came out,
so, it was 1970 or so.

their place
was this great big loft
above an old hardware store.

it was
one huge room
divided into a kitchen,
the living space,
the bathroom (hidden by a curtain)
and their work area,

where they had
an ancient printing press
that they used
to print a magazine
modeled after
Rolling Stone.

they had
no contacts,

and they had
no ads.

all they had
was guts.

i remember the time
they invited me
for spaghetti,
served on mis-matched plates,

and wine
served in jelly glasses.

it was all
so Bohemian.

i loved
everything about it.

and
they talked Kafka...

and
they talked Celine.

and
i tried
to fake it
as best as i could.

that's all
i remember
of Dan and Carol.

i

hope
they understand.

look at

all
these
wrinkles
on my face.

i love them.

i earned
them.

they're
mine.

Landon

got
drunk
on a gallon
of MD 20/20,

and
spent
the night

on the kitchen floor,

looking
for Van Gogh's

other ear.

the first

good
advice
i ever got,

was
when i
was five years old,

and my
grandfather
called me over

and said
brush your teeth
and never play with matches.

it doesn't get any better than that.

Martin accused me

of
stealing
my lines.

i told him
don't fuck with me, little boy.

you
bit off
more than
you can chew.

every time
you tell
a lie

about
me,

i'll tell
the truth
about you.

i haven't
heard a word
from him since.

okay, Mr. Death, you win...

i'm not so young and stupid
to think you haven't
stacked the deck.

you
own the house.

you
make the rules.

but, today,
the victory is mine.

today
i've fought you to a standstill.

today
i've got this poem...

this
glass of wine...

i've
got my wife...

my books...

and,
over there
i've got that stinking,
snoring dog.

that's
victory enough for me.

today, Mr. Death,
you lose...

and the glory
of the gods
is mine.

since before

we
were
forever,
we always
shared one soda
with our pizza.

that
probably
goes back to when
we were still dating
and broke as anything.

to
this day
we'll be in some
mall food court,
having our pizza
and sharing that coke.

some habits
are just too good.

to
quit.

object lesson:

when looking in
the mirror,

it's often best
to overlook

the beginnings of
a sag under
the chin,

and wrinkles
under the
eyes.

it's often best
to ignore
the gray
around the
temples,

and
the bloodshot eyes.

no,
what you
really have to
watch out for, is

that look of fear,

and

resignation.

even
terror.

it'll
kill you
every time.

"i really don't drink much,"

he said,

"not like i used to, anyway.
but when i do,
it's tequila.

straight.

i don't do shots
like some crazy kid.

i'm smarter than
that.

i just sit there
and sip.

some days
when my cousin comes
to visit –

especially in the summer –

we'll grab a bottle and some cigars
and sit out in the yard
all afternoon.

sometimes
we don't even say a word.

we'll just

sit there
and sip."

you've really got to admire that
in a man...

the ability
to relax
and ignore
approaching doom.

he died

Friday
night.

without grace,
or gallantry,
or style.

he
died

with
a tube in his nose,

his arm,
black and swollen,

and
one scrawny foot

stuck out
from under the covers.

it was
raining outside,

and
his nails
needed a trim.

for years now

my poems have been
filled with silence
and quiet times...

little stuff.

i find
i'd much rather write about
lying on the couch
with the tv off,
listening to my dog
work on a bone
while the clock ticks.

no great thoughts
or theories
or even
memorable lines.

just life.

paring things down.

stripping them
to the
bone.

minimalist stuff.

keeping that in mind,
i'm even thinking

of going downstairs
and getting rid of
all my books
with the exception of
To Kill a Mockingbird,
a dictionary
and
The Grapes of Wrath.

knowing
for damn sure certain
that in all things vital,

less
is more.

i don't know what it was

either
the crowd was wrong,

or
i was wrong...

or both.

but,
it just
wasn't working.

i read
poem after poem.

nobody laughed...

nobody clapped...

and i couldn't blame them.

i
was shit,
they were shit,

and it was
all falling apart.

the walls
stunk

and
the floor
was cracked.

when
it was over
i sold some books,
grabbed my coat, and ran.

i got in the car
and put on a cd
of me reading on another night.

that night
they got my jokes,

they
loved my poems

and
i was
handsome

and tall.

the world made sense.

but it didn't matter,
because that was then

and this is
now.

so i took out the cd
and put in one
by Hank Williams.

it was a live recording
and Hank was good.

Hank was a god
and in his entire career
he never
ever
had a bad night...

did he?

we

are
less
than
ghosts.

approaching 70:

at
this
point in the game,

i guess
i'm supposed to
be writing things like:

"sands at 70";
"the end is near";
and "ode to my lost and misspent youth"...

but,
i get the feeling
that i ain't done yet.

not
by a long shot.

so,
give me
what you got.

i'm
tough.

i
can
take it.

go

ahead.

i
double-dog dare you.

the knees

are
gone.

i no
longer drink.

my
days
of tequila
are a thing of the past.

more
often than not,
i'm in bed by nine.

steps
are a challenge.

i
have
some kid
who cuts the grass.

it's all
different now.

it
seemed
to happen overnight.

i

guess
that's just
the way it goes.

change
(like they say),

is
inevitable.

but,
the one thing
that will never change...

for
now,
at least...

after
i climb
the stairs...

after i
take my pills,

prop
the pillows,

pull
the covers,

flip
the lights...

there
will still
be me and you,

and
that dog
between us,

with
her dirty feet

and
stinking breath...

and
the rest of the world

will
have to
wait its turn.

i bought the new

Bukowski book
yesterday,
and it's
sad.

they've been picking
his bones for
sixteen years
now,

bringing out
new books
of poems
every
year,

each one getting
worse and
worse.

publishing every poem
they can get
their hands
on.

thousands of
them.

they must be
near the end, though.

this one's
hardly
more
than a hundred
pages long.

we've finally squeezed
the life out of you,
haven't we?

i guess we got
what we
wanted.

and now,

after
years of
weaker and
weaker poems
we've managed to
run you to ground...

you've finally become
what we always
wanted you
to be.

one of
us.

they tell me

i'm writing too much
about writing
lately.

in fact,
they tell me
a lot of
things.

"you're a fraud,"
they say,

"these aren't
poems,

these
are just
diary entries.

what are you
trying
to do,

pull
a fast one?"

what
i should say

is
i haven't

pulled a fast one
in years,

but
i don't.

i let it
go.

just
like i let
all the other
comments
go.

see this poem?

consider it
my one and only

fast
one

pulled
today.

now that Bukowski's dead

what are all the
wannabe's
that never were
going to do?

what are they
going to do
for inspiration?

who will they
turn to now?

who's going to tell them
how to drink,
think
or write?

who's going to tell them
that Dostoyevsky's cool...

that John Fante
had a way
with words

and that it's
a lot more fun
to stay in bed
and think about it
than it is
to have to
get up

and write about it?

now,
they'll
pick his bones
like they did
with all the others

and look for reasons
where there were
none...

and explanations
where there are none...

where (more often
than not) there's just
some slob
who lived his life
and wrote
and loved
and slept
and ate
and died.

there's
no mystery at all...

really...

just ask
Bukowski.

this poem

has
no form

no
beginning

no
end

it is
therefore

perfect

PART 2

"write a poem about *THAT*,"

she
said,

sitting
on the edge
of the
bed,

smiling.

i was reading

in the
sun room when
this annoying little fly
kept buzzing at
the screen,

trying
to get out.

unlike most flies,
he wasn't very fast
and when i swiped at him
with my hand he fell
on the floor
behind
me.

i
thought
he was dead,

but then
he shook it off

and flew
into the next room.

minutes later,
he was back at it,
still trying to get out.

still
annoying the hell out of me.

this time
i hit him with
a rolled up newspaper,

but he shook it off again.

finally,
i caught him in my hands.

i opened the door
and let him out.

he
earned it.

the tough
little bastard

earned it.

the miracle

is
not
always

what it
appears to be.

the
miracle
sometimes

is
only
smoke

and
mirrors

and
some
poor slob's
picture

of
his slightly
broken
dreams.

my old dog's gone deaf

it happened
practically
overnight.

the vet says
sometimes it
happens that way.

she's not
in any pain,

and
it doesn't
seem to bother her.

when she's
out in the yard,

and i
call her
to come in,

she
sits there,

and
stares at me.

same
as always.

sometimes,
i even forget
she can't hear me.

actually,
she never really
listened to me, anyway.

in
that respect
her behavior
hasn't changed one bit.

it seems
old habits die hard.

i'm
just glad
old dogs do, too.

i ask

the lady poet
"what are you
doing now?
what's
your ambition?"

and
she says
"i want to write.
i know i've got
great poems –
even immortal poems –
in me."

"and what
are you
doing about it?"

"oh,
i'm reading
everything i can.

preparing myself.

getting
the instrument
ready."

and i say
"yes,
but are you

writing?"

"no.
i'm not
ready for that yet.

i'm waiting
till the time's right.

waiting
for the proper
inspiration.

do you
understand?"

yes, ma'am,
i'm afraid
i do.

weep

for
Jack
Kerouac

Jesus Christ!

poetry
isn't about

perfection.

it's not about
haikus

or
sonnets
or sestinas

or
any
of that
other crap.

it's
about
taking that

corner
on two wheels

and
never
looking back.

don't put me

in
poetry
contests.

what, is it
a game with you?

fine.
keep it
to yourself.

i
don't
want to
win anything.

i don't
want to be
judged the best.

i
don't
even want
to be in the running.

i
just

want to survive.

one

more
day.

why i'm not Buk...

beyond
the talent, of course...

there's also this
to consider:

classical music
doesn't interest me...

i don't
duke it out
in the alley
with the boys
from the bar...

i don't even know
a single prostitute,
and

my face has yet
to really show
the ravage
of my
years.

yes, Bukowski had it
figured out.

over the course of time
he managed to
write like

a slumming
angel,

while
looking
like
hell.

imagine
that.

if

being
dead is
the question,

the
answer
is only a
matter of time.

the great writer

told
him to
write about

what
and who
you know,

which
made him wish

he
had more
interesting friends.

twice

this wet
and rainy summer
we got water in the basement
and i ended up
working
all night
to keep things dry.

tonight,
for the third time,
it's coming in again.

it's 3:43 in the morning
and it's coming in again.

only
right now
i'm sitting here,
taking a break.

i've got a can of soda
that i'm going to finish
and i'm also
going to read
at least
a chapter or two
of Proust.

y'see,
i've come
to the conclusion

that no matter what happens...

no matter
how little
i work,

or
how hard i work,

sooner or later
the water
will dry up,

while Proust
never
will.

expect much,

he
would say,

whenever
he was going anywhere.

this
time he was
going to the casino.

and he
said it again.

i
never
knew what
he meant by that.

i
mean,
i had an idea,

of
course,

but,
it was
just so vague.

this time
it played out right,

and
he won
twelve hundred dollars.

walking
thru the parking lot,

he
never
even saw the car.

I've

got a
bloody nose.

the
blood

is
bright,

red

and
urgent.

i
love

it.

he

said
he
did
it
to
see
the
moonlight
shining
thru
her
head.

red:

fire trucks,
stop signs,
blood.

i can't stop
listing
things

that are
red.

like your eyes
when you
cry.

picture this:

this basement
where i write
is lined with books

and where there are
no books
there are
dvd's of old movies

and
where
there are no
old movies there's

a refrigerator
filled with beer
and a cabinet
filled with
wine

put in a
bathroom and
i could easily

live down
here,

but then,
there's
the dog,
the world,

and
you.

it was

a brown house
with a wide porch.

the Connors lived there.

when i was a kid
Tommy and i
used to hide
behind the swing
and whistle
at the girl next door.

her house
was white aluminum siding
and her name was Annie.

her father worked nights
in the RCA factory
and she was
dating this guy
who looked
like Elvis.

he drove a white
Chevy
and would pick her up
on Friday nights.

Tommy and i
would scrunch down
behind the swing

and whistle
and laugh
when she looked over.

we thought
we were cool
and we knew
she was hot.

and we'd
whistle again.

eventually,
the days passed.

the
summer ended
and we gave it up.

we moved on.

what we did then,
nearly 50 years ago,

was no joke...

although
we will all
go to our graves
trying to
get it.

even my clothes

are
beginning
to smell like you.

i
leave you
somewhere

and
end up
turning around

to see
where you are

only
to realize

it's
your luck

i
smell
on my coat.

you

are
a single

blue
thought

mingling
with
my

black

if

you
think

by
not
editing
your work

you're
creating art

think
again

a word to the wise:

never
be afraid

to
piss off
your readers.

when
you start
worrying about
what they
think,

then
you might as well
pack it
in.

a hurt that scars the landscape of the soul...

that line
flashed in my mind
a minute ago...

but i didn't know
what to do with it,
so, i let it go.

i got in the car
and drove
toward the market
thinking to myself
that some things just are...

that's all.

like
the memory
of three white roses
in a short blue vase
on a winter afternoon.

there

is
nothing
sadder
than
a
dead
dog
on
the
side
of
the
road

he spent

the better part
of his entire adult life
dancing on broken glass.

hoping
against hope

(just once)

to
hear
the demon

sing.

Murray knew he

needed
something...

this time
it was a woman.

but, you know Murray,
he was never right
about anything.

with Murray,
it was always
too much,
or, too little.

so,
when he finally did
get a woman,

he never considered
the fact that
she was
crazy,

given to
cutting his clothes
with scissors,

and banging her head
on the wall.

sure,
Murray knew
he needed something,

but,
the only thing
he knew for certain

was

she wasn't
it.

and all the sick, perverted

bastards of the world
deserve to die and awful,
bloody death...

i was picking my dog up
at the vet
today
and while i was
waiting for them
to bring her out
i looked over
at the big white dog on my right
and was shocked to see
it had an ear missing
and part of its skull
was gone.

it looked like an old wound
that had healed over
and i nodded at the owner
and asked:
"what happened
to your pooch?
she get hit by a car
or something?"

"nah", he said, "she's
a rescued dog."

"rescued?"

"yeah, we found her in
the road, thrown out,
with her ear gone
and her head half torn away."

"what happened?"

"the cop said
they see it all the time.
they figure she was raised
by people who fight pit bulls,
and you can tell by looking at her
that she's real sweet,
and i guess
when she wouldn't fight
she was
probably just
used."

"used?

for what?"

"bait."

neither one of us
said a word.

i knelt down
and gave her a hug
and scratched her neck
and when i did
she turned real quick

and gave me
a great big
wet
sloppy kiss.

right on the face.

and all the sick, perverted
bastards of the world
deserve to die
an awful
bloody death.

Screaming Jay Hawkins

had a song that
mentioned
eating
cow fingers
and mosquito pie.

that was spring,
1955.

they
sure don't
write them like that

any
more.

somebody take my picture, quick!

right now
Kathy's upstairs baking something.

i don't know what it is,
but the recipe calls for whiskey.

she asked me to get it for her,
so i dug a bottle
of Jack Daniels
out of the liquor cabinet.

it's right now sitting on top of
the desk in front of me,
along with my reading glasses
and some poems i just finished.

it'd make a great picture...

the hard-drinking and harder-living
poet,
knocking off the poems
and the JD
with equal skill.

a great picture.

take it
now.

take it now, and
i'll sign it for you.

take it, now, and
i'll give you twenty bucks
to go away.

take it now,
before you go
upstairs
and take that other picture...

you know the one...

me,
in an apron,
taking cookies from the oven.

i was sitting in a corner

next to the bathroom,
and there was a phone on the wall.

it was busted,

and there were
maybe half a dozen
people at the bar;

there was this man
and a woman
who looked old
and comfortable
in the way they
leaned on their elbows
and stared
straight ahead.

every now and then
they'd make a joke
and laugh.

at the other end of the bar
was another man and woman
who were arguing loudly
about whether or not
benzedrine was a drug.

in the corner,
seated alone,
was a guy in his 50s.

he had the gut
and the smokes
and the boots.

his shirt was rolled up,

and he didn't just drink...
he DRANK.

he'd sit at the bar,
staring at his beer
for 20 minutes or so,
not moving (other than to smoke),
not touching his beer,

just looking down and thinking.

then he'd pick it up
and finish it off,
real quick.

just like that.

he'd pick it up
and polish it off...

and then he'd start all over again,
doing his thing,
looking as if
the only thing he really knows
is that the future
is never

quite
what it used to be.

contrary

to
popular opinion,

the
internet

has ruined
poetry

for
the world.

it
has fooled

too many
people

into
thinking

they
can do

this.

the dog

simply
and calmly

died.

Tony

accidentally
hit his thumb
with the hammer.

"Jesus Christ!"

Pat
looked at him
and said:

"don't get me
started...

Jesus was
nothing
but
a

scapegoat.

someone to
blame it
on.

they needed
someone
who knew the
score,

but didn't seem
to care.

he just happened to be
in the wrong place
at the wrong
time.

just
like your
god damned

thumb."

the next question

he asked
was the usual:

"so,
who's had
the most influence

on
your poetry?"

i looked at him
and said:

"Hank Williams,
Groucho Marx
and Willie Mays."

i've heard it said
the pleasures of the damned

are few
and far between.

this
was one of mine.

he clued her in

on Miles Davis,
Billie Holiday,
Knut Hamsun

and
Sarah Vaughan.

he showed her that
The Well Of Loneliness
is more than
just a book...

he played her
Sketches Of Spain,
Kind Of Blue
and every recording
Janis Joplin ever made.

he did all that
and so much
more.

and the kindest thing
she ever did
for him
was

leave.

the hell with

poetry,
poets,
writers,

workshops

and
books...

let me
tell you about
the 1961 Yankees.

when i

was
a kid

i had
a tricycle.

it
was red.

i could go
pretty fast on it.

we lived at the end of
our block.

i'd get on the bike
and go as
fast as i could,
down the street
to the other corner.

i wouldn't slow down,
and every time
i tried to turn
the corner,
i'd fall.

i'd always
tear my pants or
scrape an arm
or something,

but i always got back on,
and rode like hell
back to the
house.

i don't think i ever did
make it around the corner.

i didn't have to.

just
getting there

was
enough.

memories

are
part

of
what

we
are,

aren't they?

even

before
the hour sounds,

we
are already

sitting
with the dead.

i worked in a phone room once...

selling
light bulbs
over the phone.

can you
imagine that?

god-damn light bulbs.

it
was in
this little office
on the second floor

above
a pool room,

with
folding tables set up
with chairs and maybe 16 phones.

we each
had a stack of sheets
with names of prospects.

i
don't know
where they got the names

or
why,

because
it didn't matter.

because
no one ever bought the bulbs.

i
don't
even remember

how
we were
supposed to take an order

and
all i did
was dial the phone,

make
my pitch and
wait for them to hang up.

which they always did.

the job
lasted maybe
a couple of days
before i got tired of it

and
stopped going.

the
whole place
smelled of sweat

and
desperation

and
a certain
kind of failure
you never can forget.

i've been shit on...

this time
by a
bird
whose aim
was more direct,
on target
and effective
than any of
the critics
who
dislike me,
my poems,
my attitude,
my way of writing
or
just
my way of
seeing things.

in
fact,
this bird
should write
a book
and call it:

*"John Yamrus is in my sights...
lean, mean and as i see him".*

it's
a little long

for the title of a book,

but,
then,
this was

one
hell of a bird.

i'd tip my cap
to him,

but,
like i said...

he's
got me
in his sights.

after midnight

on any
given evening,

in no particular
order,

poets,
madmen
and drunks

are all
looking

either
for mercy,

inspiration

or
just a

good movie
on tv.

and

as
a very
respected
writer of poetry,

how
(may i ask)

do
you get
your exercise?

opening
wine bottles.

do not

force
your tired,
tarnished bonhomie

on
my
soul

i
will not

have
it

it's time

to
name

the
cliff

that
i

am
being

held
over.

the great

James M. Cain
ended
his novel
Double Indemnity

with two words:

The moon.

nothing
more

need ever
be said.

if

you
are
the
first
of us

to
die,

how
will
i
ever
laugh

again?

she works

on the production line
in a wheelchair factory,
dreaming of Proust
and Ginsberg
and what would happen
if Heathcliff
were to really
enter her life.

she keeps a web log
that's so wonderfully
inflamed
that her co-workers'
heads would explode
if they ever read it.

she's capable of discussing
Ezra Pound and maple syrup,
door handles,
Jim Morrison,
Jim Beam
and Johnny Walker.

she's studied Michaelangelo,
read "La Belle Dame Sans Merci"
and can tell you the real reason
why Rimbaud
took that shot in the leg
from Verlaine.

she's razor sharp,

read *The Razor's Edge*
and knows that
me too

is pretty much the same
as why not?

she
dreamed of college once,
and more...

but life
got in the way.

and now
she works the line,
dancing on broken candles.

happy
to be the one
who knows the sound
that one hand
clapping
makes.

the apartment

had
no heat,
no hot water
and no back door.

to
make it
interesting
two strippers
lived upstairs,

the problem was
they were nice girls.

broke,
just like us.

we ate
boiled noodles

and
very little else.

the
poems
came hard.

all

it
takes

is
time

and
time

will take

it
all

he

knew
it

as sure
as

he
knew

anything
in his
life

no
summer

is
endless

her

legs
stick
in
yr
head
like
the
23rd
psalm,

only
they
make
more
sense

old records

with their skips
and scratches
and pops,

make me feel
good.

i don't know why,
but whenever
i hear

some group
from the
'50s

singing about
unrequited
love,

young love,

true love,

or lost
love,

i feel good.

i feel calm and
complete.

i feel like
it's three in the morning,

the stars are out,
and the radio's on,
and they're
just about
to play
a song

by the one and only
Lee Andrews
and The Hearts.

for

eight
dollars
an hour
he stood
on the corner
holding that
god damned
going out of business sign.

he
had
a cooler
with a couple of
bottles of water and

when
he had to pee,
McDonald's was
right across the street.

he
hated
the sun.

he
hated
the kids
who blew their horn
and gave him the finger.

he

hated
his nineteen dollar
Payless shoes.

and
most of all
he hated the wine

which
was never
good enough

or
plenty enough.

but,
Janey
sure was
beautiful...

wasn't she?

when i was a kid

this dog showed up
on our porch.

my parents weren't
dog people,

so my father
chased it.

it was lost,
and cold
and wet,

and my father
chased it
away.

it kept coming back
and would sit
there,

looking up at
the door,
waiting.

my sister and i
wanted to
pet it,

but my father said
"no, let it

go."

finally,
it left,

and we
looked out the
window, watching it
go down the street
and out of
our lives
forever.

that
was my memory.

it was raining
then.

it's raining
now.

the

thing
you've
really
got
to
do

is
look
death
square
in
the
eye

and
stare
that
mother
down.

silly me

i'm
a pack rat.

i save everything.

i must have
at least 250 pens
saved
(just in case).

i've got
bits and pieces
of cable wire
and connectors.

curtain rods
from windows
in an old apartment.

dried flowers,
bricks,
bits of boards.

i've even got
tacked up
on the wall
right in front of me,

a veterinary appointment card
from a dog

that died two years ago.

god, i loved that dog.

the editor asked

for
a bunch
of my drinking poems.

old stuff.

he
didn't care
what they were
or where they were from

or
even
if they
had been
published before.

he
just
wanted
drinking poems.

odd,
since i haven't
had a decent drink

in
years...

not
since

the stroke
that got me
doing herbal tea
and fruit juice and water.

i've
even
learned
to like it.

kinda.

but
it's kept
me alive and
writing, so, i guess
there's no one to blame

for
all this mess,

except

you
and the wine

and
me.

i am not a writer...

writers
make things up.

they
massage the truth.

they take great pains
to give you
their version
of reality.

no,
i assure you,

i am not a
writer.

Tony wasn't very

complicated.
he wasn't politically
correct,
either.

he thought
harass
was the best part
of a woman's anatomy.

he was basically
a good guy,
though.

a guy
who liked baseball,

a good
glass of wine

and
the sound
a hard rain made
on his back porch roof.

that's just
part of the reason

i could never
figure out
why he

did it.

it
took them
several days

to
clean
the blood.

after

the
rain,

reading Kerouac,

listening
to Cole Porter
playing quiet in the room,

there's
even birds
singing outside the window.

the
only thing
missing here

is
you.

PART 3

i remember

the
porch

the
grey paint

the
swing

the
flowers

the
awning

and
the hedges.

my
god,

i
remember

the
hedges.

this

is
a place

of
whispers.

she said:

of
course,
you know,
i AM your savior...

that thing we do,
over there

is
more
important
than god, or
church or prayer.

Christ,
you're
right (he said).

come here...

and
show me
what you mean.

he had this thing

on
his nose.

i don't know
if it was a booger,
or what,

but
i couldn't
stop staring at it.

all the while
he kept talking to me
about his poems.

you see,
that's my curse,

as soon as
someone learns
what i do,

they start
telling me
about their own writing.

so he
says to me:

"yeah,
i started a

good one last night.

it's called
"The Keys To Life."

it came to me
real quick.

i bet
i'll have it
finished in a couple of weeks.

yep...
"The Keys To Life."'

i
didn't
know what to say,

but it
didn't matter...

i wasn't listening.

and
that thing
was still on his nose.

so,
i reached
in my pocket,

grabbed

my own keys to life,

got in the car
and drove
away.

if

you
can't
figure out
that my poems

have
no titles,

call
this one
ucanhaveyrfuckincityback

and put
d.a. levy's
name on it.

most days

he
just sat
with the sun
coming in over his shoulder,

like something out of
a Robert Mitchum movie.

he'd read
The Grapes Of Wrath
and play old Alberta Hunter songs

the
good ones.

the
real ones.

it
went on
just like that...

day
after day,

until
the luck

finally ran out.

and

he was
good with that.

even if

the
poems
get ignored,

the
work
gets done,

and
your life

is
saved.

nothing

helps.

one of my first

publishers
is retired
and living in France.

he's on his second wife and
lives on
a farm in the country.

every now and then
he sends me
these long, long
emails talking about the wine,
the food, the people
and how much he
loves his life
since he
ditched the
first wife, gave up writing
and moved away.

in relative terms
he's on the near side
of rich...

i swear to god
he got
none of that
from publishing
me.

i didn't even answer

his last two
emails.

i didn't know
what to say,
other than
i hope
he's happy over there,
in France,
with his
2`nd` wife and
his fields and
his wine.
when you
get right down
to it,
at the end of it all,
we both won...

he
and i...

he's got
France,

and
i've got

me.

my friend Bill

played guitar.
this was back in '72.

 or,
 maybe '73.

or,
maybe
before that,
because i don't really
remember and it doesn't really matter.

my
friend Bill
was maybe 23,
with long straight hair.

he
was skinny
and had spent time in Vietnam.

when
i first met him
he just got back from New York.

he
thought
he was a folk singer,
but, wasn't very good and
all he played were Dylan songs
and when he laughed, he kinda cackled.

Bill
would sit
in my kitchen
playing his beat up
old guitar and every now
and then he'd go out in his car

and
smoke
a joint because
my mother was in the
house and he didn't want her to know.

Bill sang thru his nose and
slammed the guitar so
hard he was always
breaking strings.

he was a good guy.

i knew him for
a year or two and then

we
lost touch.

somebody said
he spent time in the psych ward
at the VA hospital, and when he got out
he went straight to his car,
drove out to the woods
and hung himself.

Bill never
made it
big.

they found his guitar
propped against
the tree...

damn,
if it didn't
have a broken string.

"stop opening things with your teeth,"

she
said.

"number one,
you'll break a tooth.

number two...

well,
it's just a
nasty, ugly habit.
and i don't
like it,

so,
cut it out."

she
was right.

she
always is.

"besides,
when you do
something stupid like that

it makes you
look like an ass-hat."

i

couldn't
argue with
logic like that.

so,
i put it
on the table,

thinking
maybe this time

i actually bit off
more than i could chew.

first

you
dream,

then

you
die

the streets

are
dark,

and
it's not

only
the night.

tell me

a
story.

i
don't
know any stories.

tell me
a funny one.

if
i knew one,

i'd
keep it to

myself.

Ricky Lee

was
fast...

so fast,
he sometimes
didn't even leave

a
shadow.

not
that it
mattered much,

because
the things
Ricky Lee could

run from

were
never on his tail.

they were waiting for him...

right there...

patient.

at
the end

of Ricky Lee's

race.

sometimes

the
poem

asks
to not

be
written.

it's
there,

but
i

respect
its
silence.

Jesus, it

felt like
the kiss of death
when the professor wrote
and said she liked my poems
because they were amusing and irreverent

and i
wanted to
go out and shoot
myself in the back yard
just so i could break the chain

it's not
that she wasn't
a nice lady and was
paying me nicely to speak
at the school and i told her that
she should really take that money and

hire
three *real* poets instead,
as i was just a fake who got up
every morning, had my coffee, fed
the dog and came down here to fight with

the
words the
world the poems

and you.

bullets

and
bombs,

guns, injection, the chair...

heart attack, cancer,
earthquake and
flame...

there's
plenty of ways
to go,

but,
the hardest
and saddest of all

is
boredom.

they

both
knew it

do
any
one thing

long
enough

and
you'll
see things
to break your heart

the neighbor's dog

is
old

and
deaf.

she
sleeps all day,

pees
on the rug

and
throws up
every chance she gets.

i
promise
i won't do that poet thing

and
compare
myself to her.

i can't.

i'm
not deaf yet,

and
it's been weeks

since i even came close

to
peeing on the rug.

no,

i
do
not
know
who
did
this
to
me.

it was

just
another instance
of good plans gone bad.

it
didn't surprise him.

right
from the starts
he knew it was going to hell.

he'd driven
halfway to her house
behind a truckload of coffins.

he
liked
that line
from *The Great Gatsby*
that read:

"life
is much more
successfully looked at
from a single window."

he
didn't
understand it,

but,

he liked it.

he felt that
everyone should have a motto.

that
was his.

anyway,
when he got to her house,
she was already
gone.

she
finally
followed thru
on her threat to leave.

before he left,
he kicked in the back door,

walked
into the kitchen

and
looked out
a single window.

give me

wine,
my wife,
and maybe

a
dog.

that's
all i need.

and
you can
shoot me now.

her

nakedness
was
a
gift

smooth
flat
belly

white

she
kept
her
shirt
on

after working in

the yard
this morning,
my hands smell like tomatoes...

they smell like grass...

they smell like dirt
and weeds...

they smell like
an old rubber garden hose...

they smell like mulch
and sweat
and gasoline...

they smell like
my father...

and his father...

and his.

after the reading

i
took
some of the money i made

and
stopped off at K Mart...

i
bought
a bag of dog food,

some
new underwear

and
a pack of gum.

i didn't need the underwear,
and no one complained too much about my breath,

so, maybe i didn't need the gum, either.

the dog food's another story.

truth
be told,
i just wanted
to be able to spend
some of the money i made.

i

wanted
to feel that
all that standing around,
reading my poems in front of a crowd,

and
acting like a fool

was
somehow worth it.

it
didn't matter.

at
the end of the day,

they
had my books

and
i had
what little was left of my soul.

just
another
payday drunk,
hoping to make it home

before
the light turns red.

looking

at
herself
in the mirror,

she
knew
she was
a promise
she couldn't keep.

my

poems
are not meant

to
impress you.

they
are written

to
help me

make it
thru the night.

reluctantly,

he
had to accept

the
fact that

he
was destined

to
become

a
criminal

and
go to jail,

or
grow the fuck up.

there
was no middle ground.

either
way, it was

a
permanent
lack of freedom.

i never played

the
game.

i never tried to make my poems
look or sound like
poems.

never
tried writing
the big poem, and

never looked
for the one great answer.

the only thing
i ever did
well

was lean against
this wall,

trying
to look nonchalant

while Death
stared me
in the
eye.

don't

let

the
bastards

fool
you

the

sad
thing…

the
wonderful

thing…

the
glorious

thing…

is

i
don't think
i'll ever be able

to
finish
this poem.

Hardy

always
thought
he
was
too old
to die young.

circumstances soon

proved him
wrong.

i love you

at
70
miles
an
hour,

in
traffic,

on
the
Schuylkill expressway,

when
everything
around
me

has turned to

madness,

spilled wine

and
fear.

i'm

right now
sitting out back,
listening to Chet Baker –
the James Dean of 50s jazz –
and reading me some Kerouac

(*Big Sur*),

while
the sun
goes down
behind the fence
right in front of me.

how
god damn perfect

is
that?

Les Ismore

did not
appreciate
the irony of his name.

preferring
instead
to kill
a bottle of tequila
nearly every night.

he
felt he
should have been
credited
for what he saw as
excessive hipness,

but he had a hate
inside him
that
all the tequila in the world
couldn't wash away.

and less was
never ever
enuf.

midnight's

hard

it was near sunset

and there were
six of us
in the
car.

driving down
this back road,
looking for a place
to get ice cream.

we'd just
been talking about
how no one
goes for
Sunday drives
anymore.

when we were kids,
we did it
all the
time.

maybe
it was
because it was
the only thing
we could afford to do.

i don't know.

but, today,

just like the old days,
we piled into the car
and drove and
drove.

by 7:30
we had already
pointed out
nine cows,
three dogs,
two abandoned cars
and a small cemetery,
with a stone fence and
six headstones...

four of them
leaning
over,

one
already
fallen down.

we
never
did find
ice cream.

and we never
figured out
why people
don't go for drives
anymore.

but i remember thinking:
we've got
today,

and we've got
Wilson Pickett
on the radio.

that ought to be
enough.

sometimes,
the gods just
turn their heads

and look the
other
way.

he

always
said

he
wanted

nothing

and
that's
exactly

what
he

got

"everything starts right here,"

he said,
banging on
the keyboard.

"all the poems,
they all start
here."

he was like
that.

theatrical.

he liked to
put on a
show.

that was part
of the
thrill.

all that fire and
flame.

he was right,
about all
of it...

the
keyboard...

the fire...

that was all part of
what kept them
coming back,

but, the secret he
never would
tell them...

the thing that they
never could
learn,

was this:

you either
got
it,

or,
you
don't.

do not

force
your tired,
tarnished bonhomie

on
my
soul

i
will not

have
it

my friend Stanley hated the sun

he hated
the heat.

ten years ago
his wife killed herself.

she
was in a car.

i don't know
how she did it.

it doesn't matter.

my friend Stanley was
big and fat.

he kept
every room in his house
at 60 degrees.

my friend Stanley
loved dogs,
bad jokes
and beer.

my friend Stanley
is dead.

after work

i
come home,

walk
into the kitchen

and throw my wallet

on
the counter.

then
my pens,

my
cards

and
finally

my
keys,

which
slide along the counter,

spin,
do a little dance

and finally
come to a stop.

some day

so will
i.

he

was
obsessed
with Greta Garbo.

one
day in 1949
in New York City

he
saw
her.

he
told me this

himself.

New York just

wasn't
the same.

i remember
as a kid

everything
was gray and brown.

like
the old movies,

and my uncle
had this
2nd floor
walk-up,

with a
single bulb
hanging from a wire
at the top of the stairs.

i remember the night
someone
dropped
a bag of bottles
down the steps,

and the neighbors
yelled,

and my uncle
yelled
back

and
the soft grays

and
warm browns

felt safe,

and
we lounged around
in the alleys of the universe.

no, New York's not
the same.

nothing is.

except for maybe
that old girl,
sorrow.

until

a
few
days ago,

my favorite
first line
from a
novel

was the Bukowski book

that
started out:

"It began as a mistake."

now,
my favorite
first line in a novel

comes
from *Peter Pan,*

which reads:

"All children, except one, grow up."

and that's
really

the

only
mistake.

this chair

where i sit
and write my poems
is beat up and scratched,
held together with wire, tape and hope.

you figure it out.

a review

of
my latest book

laughed at
my having a poem

only
3 words long.

in
response,

i
wrote
another,

only
1 word long.

"endure"

i
figure

i'll
wait the bastards out.

Bukowski's property

this poem
isn't mine these
thoughts aren't
mine these
sentences aren't
mine these
cadences
aren't
mine
these
lines aren't
mine.
nothing
i do
or think
or write
is mine.
it's all
filtered down
through you
Mr. Bukowski...
and i wish
you'd
come here
and
take it
back.

he

sat
all day,
listening to
old Lennie Tristano records.

the dog's
bowl was empty.

outside,
the box was
filled with newspapers and mail.

he hadn't
taken a bath in a week.

life
sure was good.

he
put on
another record,

filled
the dog's bowl,

and
sat back
on the couch.

the

geese
are loud
today.

i
hear you
calling
me,

i
think.

give me poetry

that's
new.

that fails.

that
makes mistakes.

give me poetry
that you don't know
what in the world you need to name it.

give me poetry
that bleeds from the eyes

and
shouts at the world.

give me poetry
that stands naked and beaten,

with its back against the wall,
still screaming
I AM NOW!

how

were
we
to know

we
were
happy?

PART 4

i wanna tell you a story...

i
don't
know what it was...

maybe
it was living
through World War II...

maybe
it was The Depression...

but
members
of Uncle Joe's generation
always seemed to
see themselves
as part of a
collective.

a group.

it was never

i,
or me,

it was always
we or
us.

now,

Uncle Joe,
he was a story teller.

he'd
tell stories
about high school
and his two favorite teachers.

he named them
Chisel Chin
and Hatchet Face.

he
told
stories
about the war
and serving in the
same army group
as Clark Gable.

so,
a couple
of years ago,
at a family reunion,
Uncle Joe was
swapping war stories
with Uncle Leonard.

Uncle Leonard
talked about
his aircraft carrier
getting hit by
a kamikaze.

and,
these days,
with computers,
someone went downstairs
and actually found a combat photo

of
that plane
just before it
hit the
ship.

and,
these two old men...

when they saw
that picture,

with the plane
slicing through the sky...

they
stood up...

and they were
collectively

young
and tall
and strong.

i saw them

at their
finest.

and
i'll never forget it

as
long
as i live.

miracles

are
a dime
a dozen

and salvation's

just
another
one of your
bad
ideas.

what
the hell
are you talking about?

she
said as
he laid his head

down
on the bar.

nothin'...

just
talking to a guy
who
used to be
a friend of mine.

a really bad poem about a real good dog...

Phoebe's
pretty much deaf now
and can't jump up on the bed anymore.

even the steps
are getting tough for her
and she hardly has
any interest
in playing with her ball.

she still carries it with her
out of habit,
but that's about it.

now,
when she walks out into the yard to pee,
she walks slowly,
with her head down

and
she keeps
turning around
to look over her shoulder
to make sure i'm still there...

waiting.

and i stand
in the doorway

and watch

and wait.

i
owe her
that much.

it's the least i can do...

standing there,
powerless,

while slowly,
but surely,
the world slips away.

if

you ask
for my opinion

don't
get pissed

when i
give
it.

Dr. Lambert

made
house calls.

that's right.

back when i was a kid,
as part of his day,
Dr. Lambert
made house
calls.

if you were sick,
he'd come around,
check your temperature,
give you a shot,
take three bucks,

and leave.

he's dead now,
and someone else
is in his house.

they knocked down
the fence
and are painting
the place
an ugly
blue.

i drove past it

263

the other
day.

it's a mess,
and Dr. Lambert
is a memory.

i guess it's
all so simple.

all
so clear.

there are just
way too
many

of us.

something
(i'm sure)
Dr. Lambert

clearly understood.

i was out

cleaning the pool
and a spider
landed
on my
back.

it
was big,
maybe three
quarters of an inch.

i didn't know
what it was
at first,

and
thought
it was a leaf,
and brushed it off.

then
i saw it,
flailing there,
in the water, and i
splashed it out of the pool.

i don't know
if it bit
me,

but

i keep
rubbing my back,

wondering,

waiting for
my feet to swell,
my face to turn black
and the whole world
to suddenly go
dark.

when

asked
why he called
his newest book
They Never Told Me This Would Happen,

he answered:

someone already picked
Play The Piano Drunk
Like A Percussion Instrument
Until The Fingers Begin To Bleed A Bit.

so,
you see,
he had no choice.

i think

the time that
you're the most
beautiful is when
your face is swollen
from sleep, and your hair
is matted and messed and i
stand at the side of the bed, the
king of all i am and all i have and

all
i will
ever be.

he'd play

Wanda Jackson's
"Am I Even a Memory?"
over and over
again,

all
day long.

sorrow
was never
the problem.

the
problem
was Janey.

Janey
and that
thing of hers.

neither
of which
he could ever

forget.

after my colonoscopy

the
doctor
came in and
said he found nothing.

that was funny...

if you believe my critics,
i thought for sure
he'd find my
head.

Rick

was
this old
friend of mine
who gave me my first
and only award for poetry.

it was
near 3 in the morning

and we
were drunk
on cheap vodka,

complaining
how we couldn't
get published anywhere

and never
won any awards for our work

and
we were
standing on this corner

ready
to call it a night

and
he looked up
at the street sign
and saw that it was Wakefield Street

and
he handed me
the bottle and said:

i now award you
the prestigious Wakefield Prize

except
he was drunk
and couldn't say it very clear.

but,
like they
say in the books,
it's the thought that counts,

and that
was the first
and only award

i ever got

and Rick
went on to give up writing

and
playing the
piano and guitar.

and
he taught Econ
in a very well-known college

until
one day
he'd had enough

and
stuck his head

in
the oven,
looking, i suppose,
for whatever remained
of his music, his hopes, and his dreams.

Henry Miller,

James Jones,
Dos Passos,
Zola,
Kerouac,
Meyer Levin...

the thing
about it
is
they're all dead

and i'm
still here,
fighting with this poem
that won't go away.

the good thing
about it
is
there's beer
in the refrigerator,

books
on the shelf

and
a movie on tv.

that's good enough
for me.

Steinbeck and Zola
and all the rest
can have
their
immortality.

i'm more than content
to sit here and enjoy
what little is left
of mine.

Bukowski started his novel

Post Office
with the line:

"It began
as a mistake."

most things
(good and bad)
start that way.

like
this poem,
which had me
thinking about
all the crap i write every night.

most of it's
not very good,
but that's just the way it is.

that's the way
life is.

you
get up,
go to work,

come home
and go to sleep.

and

in
between

you try
desperately
to hold onto the fire.

Randolph was an ass...

he
didn't know it,

but he was an ass
all the same.

he loved to
argue.

he'd argue
about anything.

i'd call it
red,
he'd call it
black.

no matter
what i'd say,
it was
wrong,

and he had
the better
idea.

i can't say
he didn't make
perfect sense
every now and then.

there was that time
i came to him
and said
"man, this is
a great day,
isn't it?
look at
that sky.
you just gotta
smile."

and he turned to me,
like he always did,
with that
shit-eating grin
and said:

"sure,
you're happy now,

but,
don't worry,
you'll get over it."

when i was a kid, i

worked
in a shoe factory.

i was
a "heeler",

putting heels
on women's shoes.

i'd glue the heels
to the soles

and put them on
a conveyor
that took them to
a "trimmer"
who sanded the excess.

if i didn't
do it
well enough,

or
fast enough,

he'd
turn around
and throw a shoe at me.

pretty soon,
it got to be a routine.

i'd glue
and duck, and
glue and
duck.

i was young
and quick...

he rarely ever
hit me.

eventually,
the work ran out,

and i
moved on.

i often wondered
what drives a man
to act like that?

after all,
we were
piece workers.

we
got paid
by the shoe.

it
cost him money
to throw

at me.

anyway,
that was a
long, long time ago,

and
i'm sure
he's dead by now.

Leo...

his name
was
Leo.

tonight

i'm watching the ballgame
(the Phillies are down
2-1 in the 7th)...

between innings
i'm also watching
The Sands of Iwo Jima,
with John Wayne
and reading the poems of
Edna St. Vincent Millay.

one day,
between the poems
and the movies
and the ballgames,
death
will surely
beat my door in...

before that time
i hope to
read
and write
and hope and love
and walk the streets at night.

one day,
surely,
death will
beat my door in...

and
when it does...

when my back
is to the wall
i will still
wave my arms
and try my luck
at shouting down the wind.

she could have been great

she could have been
one of the ones
that mattered.

but,
she wouldn't listen.

she
thought
that just because
she wrote like a slumming god,

the
world
would beat a path

to
her door.

she
never
figured out

the world
doesn't come to you.

you

bring it

to

the world.

one
word
at a time.

that's just the way
it works.

and
in the
eyes of god,

some
prayers

are
better left

unanswered.

i sat in the sun room

reading
old books...
juvenile books, mostly.
stuff from back when i was a kid.

the
latest was
National Velvet,

the one
that got made into
a movie with Mickey Rooney
and a very young Elizabeth Taylor

back in 1944.

i remember seeing *National Velvet*
when i was in grade school.

it wasn't 1944.

it was
probably
the late '50s
and my mother
used to let me stay home
sick all the time from school.
there was even a year when i came
this close to getting held back because
i racked up so many sick days, but they couldn't
keep me back because i was quiet and had good grades

and anyway, like i said,
i used to stay home from school

while
my father
drove a delivery truck

and
my mother
worked in one of
the many dress factories
that crowded the neighborhood.

my grandparents lived right across the street,

and
my grandmother
used to come and check on me at lunch,
bringing jars
of canned cherries
from the tree they had,

and
i would sleep on the couch

watching
movies on tv,

and
i remember
National Velvet being one.

but,
i didn't
like it very much,
because there wasn't any

shooting in it,
and it was just for kids.

but,
it was the only thing on,

so i watched it.

the book
(and the movie)
is about a girl who's skinny and frail

and
a horse
that's big and tough

and
the girl wants
to run it in a race,
only the race isn't open to girls.

reading it now,
it's a pretty good book

and it
takes me back
to those days in 1959
when i got to stay home from school

and
lay on the couch
eating a great big bowl of cherries.

and i had a pillow and a blanket
and the room and the world around me was

warm
and safe
and good.

Tony The Lip

was
older than he looked,

was
impressed
by the smell of his own farts,

lied
about everything,

never
held a job for long,

ate
everything,

drank
anything,

and
changed his shorts

no
more
than once a week.

Tony had
3 bad marriages,

4 shack-ups,

and
that one month he
never cared to talk about.

i
always
liked Tony.

he

didn't
know what
he had to do next.

he
only
knew

he
had to.

it's too late

they'll never stop me now.
they should have
caught me

when i was young
and soft,

but it's too late.
now i'm old
and tough,

and no matter what they do,
they'll never catch me,

and what kills them is
they know it.

all their efforts
have always
been

too
much,
too little,

and now, for sure,
far too
late.

it's all too safe...

running
with the bulls.

sky
diving.

climbing
Mount Everest.

wrestling
alligators.

racing
cars.

catching bullets
in your teeth.

it's all
too simple.

too
safe.

just once
let one of

those guys
come down here

and try

writing

one
really honest

poem.

poetry

is
a
bloodsport
practiced
to
keep
the
wolves
from
the door
and
the
ghosts
from
the
mirror

right now,

i'm reading
War and Peace
for the umpteenth time,

The Forsyte Saga
for the first,

and
a book
on the 1889
Johnstown Flood.

i
don't know
what that says about me.

nor
do i care.

my coffee's
getting
cold.

this

is a poem
for my dog
who is 3 years
and 4 days old and
she has more spirit and
intelligence and glee in her
than anyone i will ever know.

ever.

my dog doesn't care much

for
literature.

she doesn't care
that the editors write
asking questions,
demanding
answers.

she doesn't
care
that
there's
books to be sold,

poems
to be written,

and
hands
to shake.

all she wants
is to have
her bowl
filled

her
head
scratched

and
to be
let out

when
it's time to

shit.

message read

on a
license plate

this
afternoon:

IWUVJB

for all
the money in the world

i wouldn't want to be
JB.

i was just now

out in the yard,
cleaning up,

and
i found
one of Abby's balls.

i picked it up.

and
as soon as
i threw it, i knew.

watching that ball
come to a stop
nearly broke
my heart.

he looked at me and

asked;
"in your writing,
don't you even *care*
about musicality?"

you
could feel
the sarcasm and hate
coming out of
his pores.

it was
live television
and what i should
have done
was taken a leak
on his desk,

but
i just sat there,
and stared at him,
enjoying the moment.

letting him
squirm.

it was
one of the few questions
he asked during the interview
and it didn't even deserve an answer.

after that,
he shut down completely,
and i finished the interview alone,
reading my poems
right into the camera.

it was all
quite dramatic, and
i enjoyed it.

there's something
really good about being hated.

it's
as real as rain.

when it was over,
he left,
immediately,
and i drove home,
with the radio turned off,

more than content to
listen to the sound
of distant
thunder.

doing the laundry,

i separate
the whites
and the colors...

those items
that can be
washed in hot...

and those
that must be
washed in cold.

the running washer
sounds like white noise...

oddly
comforting.

i laugh at
the uselessness of it all

as
i start
to dust.

driving toward Lancaster,

mid-afternoon,
route 222,
listening to James Brown.

James Brown,
who at times could care less for lyrics...

James, who once said:
"if you ain't got
enuf soul,
let me know,
cuz i got soul to burn".

James, sweating, singing,
dropping to the floor...

and i look out the window
to my right
and see two farmers
standing
hands on hips,
next to a dark blue pick-up,

staring down at a cow
that's wedged
up against a fence.

dead.

like it backed up
in the face of death

until it
couldn't back up
any more.

and the farmers
are probably wondering
how in hell
they're gonna get that thing
in the truck
before it rains.

and James Brown
screams:
"GOOD GOD!
HIT ME!
HIT ME!

HIT ME ONE MORE TIME!"

"Dear John:

Concerning your most recent poem...
as always, it's engaging
and technically correct,
but you're beginning to sound a bit
one-note to me.

How about trying a poem
that isn't about other people's poetry –
or, better yet,
a poem that doesn't even mention poetry?"

hi;
i'm writing to you
to let you know
i appreciate your concern
for my literary safety...
but, poems are like cookies...
sometimes you just get cravings
for one particular type.

right now,
i'm into chocolate chip.

that being said,
in taking your comments to heart,
i went back and checked...
i've sent you
exactly 39 poems,
13 of which
are about the writer's life,
or writing.

i have no real defense for that.

i'm afraid i AM a writer,
and the only subject matter i have
is me.

however,
that still gives you
26 other poems to consider.

you can also
be happy in knowing
that of those 26 poems,
there's not one mention of writing...

there are also:
zero unicorns
zero faeries
zero dappled daisies
zero mentions of cutting my wrists
zero use of the words "life sucks"
and zero poems entitled:

"Life, Love or Death."

you can also
feel confident of
finding poems that talk about
picking my nose,
going to the fridge for a beer
and watching my dog take a dump.

thanks for your continued interest...
best...
     always...
          john

the other day he

said to
me:

the
only
subjects
i have left
are sex, drinking
and the writer's life.

and
i'm sorry
to have to say

i'm now writing
better than
ever.

his book,

Scratch Yer Balls With A Brick,
was groundbreaking,
gritty
and real.

but,
after that...

after it
hit,

he had
nothing left.

empty
and desperate
he published
Screw The Pooch,

but
the readers
saw right thru it,

and
it bombed.

blocked,
and uninspired,
he decided he'd
make like Salinger
or Harper Lee

313

and go silent.

when he
did,

no one cared,

and he was
gone.

just
like that.

lately,
he's been
working as a
greeter in Walmart.

he
drinks
more than
he should...

cuts his grass,
bites his
nails,

and dreams
of days
gone
by.

his face

was odd.

tiny eyes that
squinted.

a forehead
so high

it made you
think
of

cathedrals

and

lips
that promised

laughter,
love,
or

fury.

on reading some of

my
poetry,

this
guy i knew

said
"damn,
if that's what
you call poetry...

i can do that
any time."

and he
pulled a pen
out of his pocket

and wrote:

"the birds
that fly over
my yard in the summer

never bother
to land,

they only
shit in the pool."

then,

he put the pen

back
in his pocket,

smiled

and walked
away.

she said

touch
spit to me

and
i sizzle.

that's
way too hot

he
said.

damn it,
pass the tequila.

i'm a sucker for

black and white
movies.

and salads made with
oil and vinegar.

and real crunchy
garlic bread.

i have a high tolerance for pain,
except for needles
and hangnails.

i love dogs,
hate cats,

and slam the door
on Jehovah's Witnesses.

i like
W.C. Fields,
Groucho Marx,
fart jokes
and anything
that has to do
with World War II.

i've had
five great
loves in my life.

four were
dogs.

the fifth
is upstairs,
laying on the couch,

half
asleep,

watching *Dateline*.

she

looked at
him and said:

"you're enough".

"enough for what?"

"for me."

with that,
she lay back

and
smiled.

they
never heard

the
rain.

my car battery died and

i was
waiting
for Triple A.

i thought
i'd kill some time
by writing a bit.

nothing came,
so, i
gave it up,
did the dishes,
played with
the dog and
waited,

thinking
it's just like life,
isn't it?

you do your
thing,

then
sit around
waiting
for the truck

to take you
away.

find

the
poem,

eat
the words,

and
carry on.

i'll

tell you one thing
for certain...

i've got a lot more
yesterdays

than
tomorrows.

the
only thing

good
about that

is
they
all were spent

with you.

i think

i was
28 at the time
and was in California
to do some readings and promote
this really bad novel i had just published

and
they put me up
at a place called Sally's Motel

somewhere
out in Long Beach.

Sally's
had this little
u-shaped courtyard
that surrounded the pool

which
was empty
except for the cracks
and the weeds and the dirt

and
the shame,

and
my room
had two grimy beds
and a tv with a coat hanger antenna.

Sally's
was on its last legs back then,

and
i'm sure
Sally was, too.

there actually *was* a Sally

and
she looked
just like you would have pictured her,

with
the bleached blonde hair
and the cigarette jammed between her bright red lips

and
the lobby
looked like every other lobby

in every
other sad motel.

it was
just this little hole of a room

and
just behind the room
you could see where Sally lived

and
the tv was on

and the whole place
smelled of whiskey, smoke and
some poor old dope's broken, shattered dreams.

the neighbor died today

cancer.

she lived
with
it

nobly

and
long.

just
not
long
enough.

she said

she
was pleased
to finally meet
a "genuine" author.

"i
write
a little, myself,"

she
said...

"and
one day
i'm gonna
publish a book

that's
gonna knock
everyone's socks off.

including
yours."

she
looked sad

and
asked

"exactly

what kind of writer

are you?"

i
signed
the book...

handed
it to her, and

walking away
mumbled:

the
failed kind.

i

saw
the ghost
of Etta James

driving
a blue Toyota.

i tipped
my imaginary hat

and
smiled.

it
made
my day.

my

cries
of urgency,

fear

and
remorse,

are
heard

only
by ghosts.

the doorbell rang

it was a
Jehovah's Witness,
knocking on doors
trying to spread the word.

this time
it was a young
woman in
sandals.

she
asked me
if i had the time
to answer eight questions.

i told her i was
sorry, but, i
was busy.

she said
"can you answer
just one?"

"sure."

she
asked me
to tell her what i
believed.

i said:

"two things...

Jerry Lee Lewis
is the father of Rock and Roll,

and knocking on my door
is a monumental
waste of
time.

mine
and yours."

if

you
want
your poems

to
be
real,

live them,

don't
write them.

i'm getting mean,

and i don't like it,
but i just can't take all the
bad poetry i'm seeing.

i know i should stop looking,
because there's nothing good
out there...

nothing with heart and guts and soul,
but i keep on looking.

and i get the letters...

"my son's a writer.
he's had some things published
in 2 online magazines
and he intends to be a poet.

he's written sonnets
and has the most absolutely lovely
rhymes.

i feel so good
and special and
sweet
when i read his things.

i even told him
he should send some of his
poems
to Hallmark,

they're that good.

i'm just writing to you because
i heard you're
a poet also.

even though
i never read any of your poems
i just had to tell you
that he wants to be a poet
in the worst way
and i'm writing to you
to hear what you had to say."

dear ma'am, it's too late...
i received your letter this morning
concerning your son
wanting to be a poet in the worst way...

i'm afraid
he already is.

the only thing

dumber
than a writer,

is
someone
who admits
to being a writer.

i am
5 foot 7,

63
years old,

and i
love dogs.

i am
not dumb,

and
i admit

nothing.

she said

you
think
that silly,
stupid grin
makes you bulletproof,

don't you?

then,
just to be

a
bitch,
she went
and proved him

wrong.

there's a poem

in
here,
somewhere.

he asked me

how do i write a poem, and
when do i know
that it's done.

that was a
fair enough question,

so i gave him
a fair enough answer.

i told him
that i write it all down.

i write it all
down

and
start cutting.

i keep cutting
till i hit
bone,

and
when i do,

there's your
poem.

Q

she told
me

she'd send
me

a
letter

i

am
here

with my
pain

and
you

are
there

with
yours

pass

the
lightning,

please.

PART 5

endure

"endure"

--John Yamrus

ACKNOWLEDGEMENTS

Some of these poems originally appeared in the following print and electronic books, magazines and anthologies: *Bayou Review, Beat The Dust, Boston Poetry, Carnival Lit, Chiron Review, Clock Radio, Cultural Weekly, Daily Dope Fiend, Degenerate Literature, Elephant, Epic Rites Journal, Epic Rites Review, Every Reason, Fekt, Fluorescent Stilts For Your Uncle, Gutter Eloquence, Heroin Love Songs, Indigent a la Carte, Into The Void, Kiss My Poetry, Lummox Journal, Mad Rush, Mas Tequila Review, Meat For Tea, Metropolis, Open Arts Forum, Orange Room Review, Outlaw Poetry, Penman Review, Pigeonbike, Preoccupied With Austin, Queen Mob, Ramingo's Porch, Rat Creek Press, Rogues Of The Red Baron Bar, Rufous, Sacramento Poetry, Short Story Library, St. Vitus, Street Poet Review, Superheroes, The Australian Times, The Exuberant Ashtray,The Smoking Typewriter, The Valley Review, Toledo Free Press, Tree Killer Ink, Unadorned Reader, Unokudo, Unrorean, Word Fountain, Zygote In My Coffee, 1/25, 12 Shotgun Blasts From The Underground*

355

ABOUT THE AUTHOR

In a career spanning more than 50 years as a working writer, John Yamrus has published 28 volumes of poetry, two novels, three volumes of non-fiction, and a children's book. He has also had more than 2,500 poems published in magazines and anthologies around the world. Selections of his work have been translated into several languages, including Spanish, Swedish, French, Japanese, Italian, Romanian, Albanian, Estonian and Bengali. His poetry is taught in numerous colleges and universities.

ABOUT THE EDITOR

Mish (Eileen) Murphy is an editor, poet, book reviewer, and visual artist. She is Associate Poetry Editor for *Cultural Daily,* an online arts magazine. She has a B.A. from New College (Sarasota, FL) and an M.A. from Columbia College, Chicago. She teaches English/Literature online at Polk State College (Lakeland, FL). Her poetry has been widely published in journals such as *Thirteen Myna Birds, Rogue Agent, Tinderbox, Writing in a Woman's Voice,* and many others. She has published four books: her debut poetry collection was *Fortune Written on Wet Grass* (2020). She also wrote *Evil Me,* a poetry chapbook (2020). Her latest poetry collection is *Sex & Ketchup* (2021). She also illustrated the highly-acclaimed children's book *Phoebe and Ito are dogs,* written by John Yamrus. Mish lives near Tampa with her husband and dog Cookie.

Made in the USA
Columbia, SC
28 June 2021

41114948R00211